P9-CQV-725

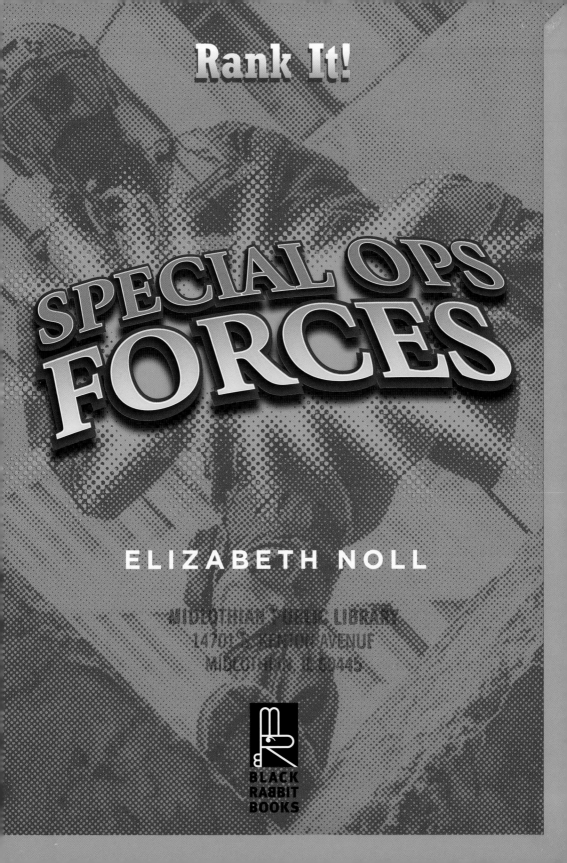

Rank It!

SPECIAL OPS FORCES

ELIZABETH NOLL

BLACK
RABBIT
BOOKS

Bolt is published by Black Rabbit Books
P.O. Box 3263, Mankato, Minnesota, 56002.
www.blackrabbitbooks.com
Copyright © 2017 Black Rabbit Books

Design and Production by Michael Sellner
Photo Research by Rhonda Milbrett

Library of Congress Control Number: 2015954679

HC ISBN: 978-1-68072-063-1   PB ISBN: 978-1-68072-269-7

Printed in the United States at CG Book Printers,
North Mankato, Minnesota, 56003. PO #1791 4/16

Web addresses included in this book were working and appropriate at the time of publication. The publisher is not responsible for broken or changed links.

BOLT

Image Credits

americanspecialops.com: Thomas W. Provost, 27; U.S. Army Photo by Pfc. Rashene Mincy, 14–15; U.S. Army photo by Spc. Steven Hitchcock, 24–25; AP: Andrey Nekrasov/Solent News/REX, 21; MAYA ALLERUZZO, 16; Corbis: Cover; Flicker: Makarov771, 19; istock: Dmitry_Schekochihin, 6; zabelin, 1, 4–5; Newscom: Boris Roessler, 13; Shutterstock: 19srb81, 16, 27 (camo); BennyFortman, 29; Digital Storm, 22; freestyle images, 10 (knife); igorlale, 16–17, 26–27, 28 (rifle); KANIN.studio, 3; Makhnach_S, 6, 9, 12, 18, 21 (sniper sight); Oleg Zabielin, 31; Pisit Rapitpunt, 10 (handgun); Vartanov Anatoly, 10 (rifle); talkingproud.us: 9; thebrigade.com, 20; Wikimedia: Israel Defense Forces, 8; United States Navy SEALs, 10 (SEAL), 32

Every effort has been made to contact copyright holders for material reproduced in this book. Any omissions will be rectified in subsequent printings if notice is given to the publisher.

CONTENTS

CHAPTER 1

Secret

MISSIONS

Special operations forces are the best of the best. They fight **terrorists**. They carry out secret missions. How do teams around the world stack up? Turn the page to find out.

RANK IT!

64 YEARS FORCE HAS OPERATED

SOLDIERS WHO COMPLETE TRAINING
ABOUT **30%**

LENGTH OF TRAINING ABOUT **47** WEEKS

CHAPTER 2

SPECIAL OPS FORCES

Green Berets
from the United States

The Green Berets are a unit in the U.S. Army. Members rescue **hostages**. They also secretly stop enemy attacks.

Very few people make it through the training. Soldiers get less than five hours of sleep each night. They push their bodies to the limit.

Sayeret Matkal
from Israel

Sayeret Matkal is one of the most feared teams in the world. It is also one of the most secretive. Team members are experts in **disguise**. They blend in wherever they go. Then they strike fast and fade away.

59 YEARS FORCE HAS OPERATED

SOLDIERS WHO COMPLETE TRAINING
TOP SECRET

LENGTH OF TRAINING
ABOUT **75** WEEKS

Joint Task Force 2
from Canada

Joint Task Force 2 (JTF2) fights terrorists. JTF2 soldiers have fought in many countries. But few people know all the places they've worked.

RANK IT!

23 YEARS FORCE HAS OPERATED

SOLDIERS WHO COMPLETE TRAINING ABOUT **10%**

LENGTH OF TRAINING **TOP SECRET**

SEAL Weapons

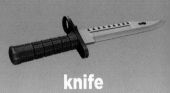

assault rifle with
grenade launcher

handgun

knife

Navy SEALs
from the United States

The word "SEAL" stands for sea, air, and land. Navy SEALs do missions in all those places.

SEAL training is very tough. Soldiers must swim with hands and feet tied. They also learn to **defuse** bombs.

RANK IT!

54 YEARS FORCE HAS OPERATED

LENGTH OF TRAINING

SOLDIERS WHO COMPLETE TRAINING ABOUT 20%

ABOUT WEEKS 30

GSG 9
from Germany

GSG 9 soldiers are highly trained police. They rescue hostages. In 1977, enemies took over a plane. GSG 9 soldiers lit a fire in front of the plane. The fire **distracted** the enemy. Then more soldiers rushed into the plane. They saved all 90 people on board.

RANK IT!

43 YEARS FORCE HAS OPERATED

SOLDIERS WHO COMPLETE TRAINING ABOUT 20%

LENGTH OF TRAINING ABOUT 25 WEEKS

SPECIAL OPS GEAR

On missions, special ops soldiers bring the gear they need.

BULLETPROOF VEST

EXTRA AMMO

HELMET

GLOVES

ASSAULT RIFLE

SPECIAL OPS FORCES

Delta Force
from the United States

Very little is known about Delta Force. It's a top secret unit. Soldiers in this group don't wear uniforms. Enemies don't know they're in the military.

Delta Force soldiers train to shoot moving targets. They also learn spy skills and how to make bombs.

RANK IT!

39 YEARS FORCE HAS **OPERATED**

LENGTH OF TRAINING

SOLDIERS WHO COMPLETE TRAINING **5 TO 10%**

ABOUT **WEEKS 26**

22 SAS Regiment
from Great Britain

The 22 SAS team is tough. Soldiers must travel 40 miles (64 kilometers) through mountains in 20 hours. They learn to survive in the jungle. They also learn to avoid being caught.

RANK IT!

75 YEARS FORCE HAS OPERATED

SOLDIERS WHO COMPLETE TRAINING
ABOUT **15%**

LENGTH OF TRAINING ABOUT **26** WEEKS

SAS
stands for
**Special
Air
Service**

GIGN
from France

The GIGN is famous for rescues. Members are also known as sharp shooters. Training for this group is tough. They practice hand-to-hand **combat** with their teammates.

RANK IT!

42 YEARS FORCE HAS OPERATED

SOLDIERS WHO COMPLETE TRAINING **5 TO 8%**

LENGTH OF TRAINING ABOUT **32** WEEKS

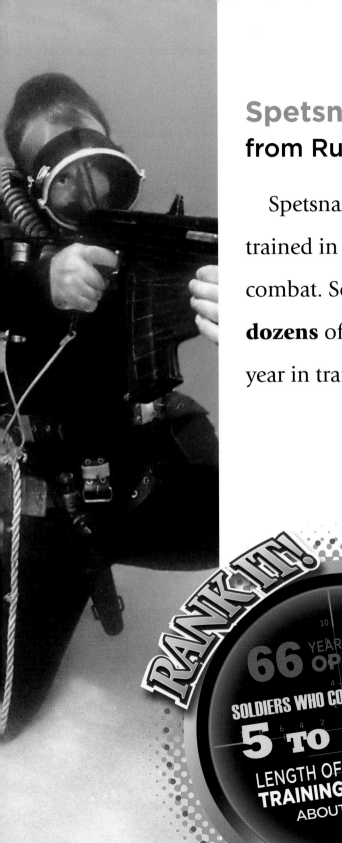

Spetsnaz
from Russia

Spetsnaz soldiers are trained in underwater combat. Some people say **dozens** of men die every year in training.

HOT SPOTS FOR SPECIAL OPS

Special ops teams work all around the world.

HAITI

CENTRAL AMERICA

AFGHANISTAN

IRAQ

PAKISTAN

YEMEN

AFRICA

RANK IT!

73 YEARS FORCE HAS **OPERATED**

LENGTH OF **TRAINING**

SOLDIERS WHO COMPLETE TRAINING **ABOUT 45%**

ABOUT **WEEKS 9**

Army Rangers
from the United States

Army Rangers are best at surprise strikes. They can take over enemy airports. They are also good at rescue missions. Rangers can be ready to fight anywhere in 18 hours.

Ranger training is tough. One part includes training in swamps with poisonous snakes.

Marine Corps Special Operations Command
from the United States

Marine Corps Special Operations Command (MARSOC) fights terrorists. Soldiers have worked in Africa, Guam, and the **Middle East**.

MARSOC training is hard. Soldiers learn to survive with little gear. They must also show they can escape enemies.

RANK IT!

10 YEARS FORCE HAS OPERATED

SOLDIERS WHO COMPLETE TRAINING
TOP SECRET

LENGTH OF **TRAINING 43-52** WEEKS

CHAPTER 3

Training

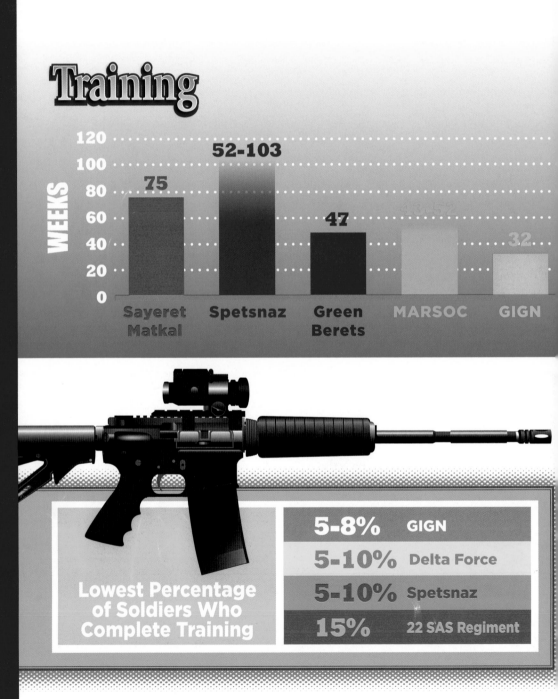

WEEKS

75	52-103	47	43-57	32
Sayeret Matkal	Spetsnaz	Green Berets	MARSOC	GIGN

Lowest Percentage of Soldiers Who Complete Training

5-8%	GIGN
5-10%	Delta Force
5-10%	Spetsnaz
15%	22 SAS Regiment

RANK IT!

Here's how the units rank.

all stats accurate as of 2015

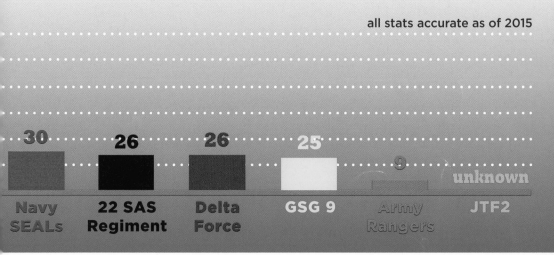

30	26	26	25	9	unknown
Navy SEALs	22 SAS Regiment	Delta Force	GSG 9	Army Rangers	JTF2

Most Years in Operation

75 — 22 SAS Regiment

73 — Army Rangers

66 — Spetsnaz

GLOSSARY

combat (kahm-BAT)—active fighting, often in a war

defuse (di-FYOOZ)—to remove the part of a bomb that makes it explode

disguise (dis-GYZ)—to change the usual appearance of someone or something so that people won't recognize it

distract (dee-STRAKT)—to take attention away from someone or something

dozen (DUH-zen)—a group of 12

hostage (HAHS-tij)—a person captured by someone else

Middle East (MID-uhl EEST)—the countries of southwest Asia and North Africa

terrorist (TAHR-ur-ist)—a person who uses violent acts to frighten people in order to achieve a goal

BOOKS

Bozzo, Linda. *Delta Force*. Serving in the Military. Mankato, MN: Amicus, 2015.

Gordon, Nick. *Army Rangers*. U.S. Military. Minneapolis: Bellwether Media, 2013.

Whiting, Jim. *Green Berets*. U.S. Special Forces. Mankato, MN: Creative Education, 2015.

WEBSITES

Navy SEALs
www.sealswcc.com/seal-default.html

U.S. Army Rangers
www.army.mil/ranger/

U.S. Army Special Forces
www.goarmy.com/special-forces.html

INDEX